BOWLING PIN FIRE

BOWLING PIN FIRE

ANDY QUAN

John Barton, Editor

Signature
EDITIONS

Cover design by Doowah Design.
Cover photos by Andy Quan.
Photo of Andy Quan by Fred Kroh.

This book was printed on Ancient Forest Friendly paper.
Printed and bound in Canada by Marquis Book Printing Inc.

We acknowledge the support of The Canada Council for the Arts and the Manitoba Arts Council for our publishing program.

Library and Archives Canada Cataloguing in Publication

Quan, Andy
Bowling pin fire / Andy Quan.

Poems.
ISBN 978-1-897109-22-9

I. Title.

PS8583.U3318B69 2007 C811'.6 C2007-905773-X

Signature Editions
P.O. Box 206, RPO Corydon, Winnipeg, Manitoba, R3M 3S7
www.signature-editions.com

for Stevie

Table of Contents

What We Live With

All You're After

Speaking Your Poetry Aloud

What We Live With

Quiet and Odd

Darren Lee and I were superstars, unafraid to swing
from the highest branch of his backyard's gnarled
apple tree, we terrorized insects, older
high-school kids, made snarky remarks about
Mrs. Kopinski in the corner house simply because
we could. We sang: *Jesus Christ /*
Superstar / Who in the hell do you think you are.

"What a shame," adults told us. We couldn't speak
our ancestral language. Nor could our mothers! Tell
them they've lost *their* heritage. What's the use anyway
of those clattery loud towers of nine tones, building
blocks flung at you in too-bright colours?

Besides, we were not Bennett Ho whose mother
banned him from sex-education class, not Adrian
Tong with his rice-bowl haircut (the fringe swinging
round his head like a carousel of animals). Brian Tom
not yet into his teens expected only bad things in life
so as never to be disappointed. Not Jacob Chiu
whose mom shaved his skull, everyone wanted to
feel its tiny combs against their fingers. Dominic
Kong was certainly not us, he told people he didn't
know Chinese but who could follow his broken
English? Definitely not Joseph Fong who stepped
in dog poop and didn't care, the playground
suddenly the Titanic sinking, passengers wailed
ABANDON SHIP!
                                        It wasn't just that they were odd.
They were quiet boys. Not like us, nails on chalk
boards, fire drill alarms: when my voice broke
I couldn't even whisper without getting in trouble.
We reckoned their tongues got caught on the way
out of their mouths like jackets on doorknobs
as they rushed outside, their mothers calling them
back to do their homework, mind their grandmothers,
though even they'd pretend they couldn't hear
or understand whatever language shouted after them.

Like a girl

It's okay, the girls told
our teacher.
And even if they come for us,
we've got Andy.

Memory fails why
or how the girls
in kindergarten knew
if approached
I could let loose
a banshee's holler, if
picked up, would
scratch out their eyes,
pinch, scream, and kick,
they were in for trouble
whoever *they* were.

Our teacher eyed me

with something much
like the fear she'd
wished to pass onto us.

Elementary

i. Recess

Now: a part of the architecture, an oddly
curved room, a window bay, a door in
shadow. Then: a frantic trading of hockey
cards, a quick round of tetherball, metal
fences to climb, games of marbles, new
ways devised to taunt the monitors, a
scout of the latest dog shit, a race around
the school. All the ways to use twenty
minutes. We'd fill them every day.
Now: a rare word, a curio by accident
pushed out of sight.

ii. Twosome

Out of nowhere: the fact of them
appearing warns us there are other
schools besides ours. *Why come here*?
One sickly, pale cheeks flush with blood,
unfortunately smart, his nose running
in cold weather; his best friend slightly
awkward, a girlish voice. Our low-
bosomed, big-bummed teacher
married to a man in a wheelchair
locks us in one recess:

Why are none of you being nice?

In place of excuses, we offer too many
explanations. Of giggles and snot, of
how weird they are. Mrs. Wiser has
nothing to say. Whatever our future
suffering, these days own theirs, long
and ghastly, knobbly-kneed, ghost
ribs still showing.

iii. Activity

Quick: we spill out of the ill-lit halls
gasping at the white mid-morning,
fall down the boys' set of stairs.
It is the week the crane flies multiply,
their twig-bodies suspended
between legs gangly as grass,
thin as nerve endings,
clinging to the once yellow
walls (paint like dandruff
crumbling), small
uncombed tufts of hair, easy
to grasp between thumb
and forefinger, the buzz
of wings like static
electricity, a solid form blurs,
becomes invisible. We
meet at the hay bales of
cobwebs where the stairs' base
joins the wall, take turns
releasing our prey, two seconds
of flight then snared again,
burrs in a sock, the thick
punctuation marks of the spiders,
torsos converging, trailing
silk, the crane flies wrapped
tight until they become still.

Spit

Traffic backed up on the Second Narrows Bridge, they'd
closed our lane and made us merge, I saw the car swing
up beside ours. My seven-year-old mouth cried *don't*
let him in. You inched forward a hand's width, so tiny
a provocation to cause such honking and shouting.
The moustached man, sleek and muscled, eyes narrow, leapt
out, cursing, yelling, engine running. Then you were
circling each other, a dance of men. He spat on the hood
of our station wagon. You tried to match his mark, spit
forming at your lips, but it was not in you to. He grabbed
your placid businessman's wrist, pinned it against your belly.
I don't know who was trying to hit or defend, the man's face
crayoned with rage. He saw me and let go. Swore one last
time. We shut ourselves back in, could not speak, his
saliva still not dry, its separate bubbles like sad
jewels or the eyes of an insect. I felt your shame,
I, who had perhaps saved you, who had caused all this.

Reprimand

I never knew her
she died before my birth
words about her were scarce
what they say about Asian women

I looked at the solemn face
in the black-and-white portrait
and thought: silent, devoted

they thought this about me too
quiet, well-behaved
conscientious, responsible

after, when I became loud
and behaved badly
grabbing the world by its throat

she raged out of her frame
loud and obstinate
in clattering village words

shouting, berating me
though I'd lost
the language, I understood

I was never like that.

Like a boy

It was some smart-arse thing I didn't even
know I'd said when we showed Kits Beach to
the exchange students from Montreal. It was
a little rundown but quiet before the long
horizon, the North Shore apartments caught
at the mountains' feet, with logs ordered
on sand imported from somewhere else.
We were four thirteen-year olds against three—
two older boys, seventeen, maybe eighteen,
one pale with straggly hair, tall, gangly;
the other stocky and dark; both wearing jean
jackets and faded Levis, worn white
T-shirts. It was the girl who charged me,
a ghost, a fury, wild eyes flashing
like the tiger's in the black-felt painting
I'd won at the PNE. *What? What*
did you say? She was as young as us.
Her protectors shoved away my friends.
She dropped her cigarette, started
swinging. *What you said. It was something.*
I leaned back against her tiny blows, arms
useless at my sides. No blood, nothing
broke. Still, before the three shot away,
dancing across the sand, her small
pink fist reached and caught my eye,
next morning it would swell and blacken.
I couldn't remember what I'd said if I had
said anything, though I might have, all
I could think at the time was *I can't hit a girl.*

Smelt

High tide. The bucket fills. The level
of slippery flesh rises with
the eyebrows of curious passersby.

He's learnt how from Ed Hong-Louie
and now, on his own, brings
his sons out to the shores
of Vancouver's harbours in late summer.

Off-season, the nets hang ignored
in our garage, tiny ribbons of green
and black algae drying into threads,
only to be shaken alive and thrown
into the boxy station wagon
(over the years a series: forest, tan,
deep blue with fake wood panelling)
the days when at last the smelt run,

the seawall at English Bay superior
to the beach at Spanish Banks—the
hip waders stay dry, the nets thrown
to length settle into perfect form.
Three brothers unhook crimson injured
gills onto concrete unsullied by sand.

They see the task ahead: stripping
nets clean of salt with the garden hose,
scaling (dull hard snowflakes everywhere)
gutting —a sharp incision coaxing
out the bloody insides (success
if they slide into the sink whole.)

Over to Mother: a quick rinse, a pat dry,

a dusting of flour and into boiling oil,
tiny eyes harden, tin-foil skin blisters;
fry them hot enough and their bones
melt into the grain of the smelt's body—

but I'm jumping ahead to the long
vivid premonitions of children—
the evening not yet done, the nets
about to be cast one last time.
Small floats dance on the grey-black
surface, drop a curtain over
the glittery school below
on the days when smelt still run.

The moon's open silver eye crosses
above, leaving dim city stars in its trail.
Father pulls in his nets, arm over arm,
lifts them to shore. We rush to collect
the last gasping shards of white.

Aftertaste

Cantonese at home, English at school
sometimes mixing, music into speech
rising falling round syllabics tumbled
into languorous stretched monotones:
shrimp pork dumplings into noodle soup
        Two wonton meins and one bak choy
        with oyster sauce. To go. Please.

Their English names were transformed
in their parents' mouths — *mai goh, soo san.*
At twelve and thirteen
Michael and Susan stopped speaking
the language of their near and far ancestors.

As adults, this tongue stilled in their jaws
their ears grasp only infant fragments
from the words drifting like kites
between their elders, only able
to order dishes in restaurants
impressing their friends, even themselves

haam yee chow faan, toong sau dofu
the sharp clicking chopsticks lift grains of rice
draw strokes and dashes of unmouthed characters
salt-fish fried rice, deep-fried tofu
leave an aftertaste they mistake for MSG.

Bowling Pin Fire

The secret connections between Chinese fathers.
Grocer, banker, mechanic, photographer, bowling
alley proprietor. Their exchanges inexact: a carton
of this season's first mangoes, a queue-jump to settle
a mortgage, a replacement muffler, professional
portraiture. Quality was scrimped only when all
agreed which corners to cut. The Spanish call it
enchufe — a socket when filled poured more
delicious currents of electricity. And flow it did
from one family to another. I tried keeping track
of Father's cronies — my map remains a crayon sketch
gone amok, the wax outlines losing shape. My own
network is unanchored and rootless. My friends stop
at random airports, fight to pay for meals. We email
and skype. I seldom know where they live.

I grew up on Valley Drive sharing space with glass
fishing balls, an ox-blood Ming vase, a painting
of Dad's childhood home, another of teen-aged mom,
porcupine fish—inflated, dried, and hung from ceilings,
Bill Reid prints, tiny baskets from far-flung tribes.
Our names marking our bedrooms. The living room
fireplace not often used, Vancouver winters too
mild. We seldom gathered there, burnt only
wood from someone's backyard, the deconstructed
frame of a neighbour's toolshed, pinecones dipped in
a crumbling chemical the texture of icing sugar
with a tint of green food colouring. They glowed
emerald, then pumpkin orange, tiny bombs of light.

Bowling pins of fine maple burned best,
you could imagine the solid hard knocking
at the end of childhood, a perfect *crack:*
a punctured sphere thrown down the alley,
velocity gathering, knocking down ten stoic little men
cross-dressed in white plastic to resist
chipping and splinters, jaunty red diamonds
emblazoned on their mid-sections, a skimpy wrap.
Retired from service, they reclined in the embers.
Sensing danger in such display, I avoided
inhaling, auras bubbling off the pins, rising
in vermilion and silver heat up the chimney
the bricks climbing away, such strange kindling.

Les Sentinelles

At the riverside beach, the *éleves* from the summer
French immersion school: we'd been allowed
time at the *épicerie* to choose our fare: *paté, crétons,*
lardons, baguettes, and small bottles of cheap
vin no one would sell elsewhere in Canada.
Jen was the first to see it, alerted the group leaders.
With sudden false cheer, we warned off the others
farther down the shore and ate without hunger.
Our faulty second tongues guessed at a history:
a pair of pants filled up with sand, the hump
of an animal, a forgotten picnic blanket anchored
by the tide. Days later we found out who it was:
a woman with a past, middle-aged, half-
deranged, disappeared to reappear to us, partial
slope of a back in something plaid, a small circle
of hair—the back of her head, a smooth rump
clothed in jeans, one shiny coin of brown skin
exposed through a rip. So little of her touched air.
It was a first for me, for most. We weren't even sure
of the words, discovered *corpse* and *cadaver* translate
only to *le cadavre*. Before we left the beach that day,
I balanced a large flat stone on my wrist. The side
unexposed to the sun felt cool, almost wet. After
proving its gravity, it asked to be put back down.

What we live with

His testing kit reminded me of a box of Crayola crayons,
the deluxe pack of sixty-four, and even then, I wondered
who had come up with all the names and who'd
arranged them as they were. These were vials not wax,
filled with the usual antigens that cause humans
to react, he said. But still I had questions, pushed
forward by the same impulse that makes me write,
a stupid grinned mystification at how everything
works. He made a scratch on my arms for each bottle,
a needle-thin chalk mark that did not draw blood. As he
ran the tests (a drop of this, a drop of that) I reacted
to so much, my arms lashed out in jumpy itching,
tiny welts rising on my skin like birthday candles:
grass, moulds, cat fur, dust mites, ragweed. Nothing
serious, my body not quite suited for the world I live in.

Mushrooms

Uncertain: would too much heat alter
active ingredients, dilute the effect?
Advice: a stir-fry, maybe an omelette,
or else the contents of the sandwich bag,
tiny pieces of the shrivelled hands of old
ladies would be inedible. So I brewed
a tea—like consommé, we laughed
and went for a stroll in a nearby park.
It was spring, just, the last year
of our degrees, the ground gone
soggy from what we thought was hard
labour (in the library carrels, faces pressed
into textbooks, vagrant eddies of calcite
—our professors still used chalk).
We roamed from tree to tree, their silhouettes
sharp and stark against a deep warm blue
night, a perfume of things unfolding
and drying out. It took me in waves,
the first, a moving screen of northern
lights wrapped around my head (*are you
OK?* I had stopped in one place, my face
tilted sideways). Next I was taking flight,
my ears extending to wings, my eyes
forward windows. I truly did feel
lifted. Absorbed in myself like leaves
steeping in water, I had no idea what
the others saw, but we climbed the high
fence behind our house, the neighbours
we'd never met, the yard we never knew
existed. Who would expect to find it
abandoned, the lawn untouched for how
long? It grew up around forsaken
machinery, constructs we forgot
the purpose for as we lay on our backs
and made snow angels in the grass.

Commotion

We got word at the lighthouse,
boarded a worn speedboat,
headed out to open waters.
This was before rumours and
radios shut in pods with nets
of cameras and gawkers.
We were alone, startled
by a glint of black and white.
An abrupt fin arcing
above lead-grey waves
and something smaller, a
butterfly, a flash of pure
energy, sun on water, on
the skin of a young orca.
We knew we shouldn't
but trailed at speed, cut
the motor, waited. Gasped.
The mother swam right
beneath us, her breadth
wider than ours, her calf
leapt up beside us, appearing
to wave. Phil at the helm,
Keith with his camera, me
on my knees, breathless.
We swore it spoke to us.
We came to in commotion
as if the centre of a clock.
Time at a distance, morning,
noon, dusk, evening, midnight:
killer whales, all around us.

The First

No one knew why, while driving home, you swerved
into the path of an oncoming truck. Sleep? A bee?
It was the summer
between two years of college. Bad news raced across
cities, provinces. We were travelling the whole
long waistline of the continent and meant to stay
with you but saw you buried instead.
It was such a small island.
Every piece of it grieved. Everyone knew you,
your family, the man who drove the truck. I knew you
least but was overcome. The Catholic service confused me.
I felt we should scream until the air around us shook,
the walls of the church collapsed, the pitch of our agony
bursting blood vessels.
I still wonder at how
I clawed into the narrative of death, how you stayed
with me, how I turned into one of those men
who drag around melancholy and nostalgia,
luggage too heavy to be allowed on board.
Returning to
classes that fall, we were quiet with new knowledge.
Roxane found a soft red plaid shirt
of yours, gave it to me. It really was very plain,
I marvelled for years whenever I wore it
how friends would comment.
I never thought
my way into the future, who else would be
lost. Looking back, you were the first.

All You're After

Red Joni Blue

A red lit through from below: darker crimson
on the underside, a planet glowing around
its circumference, the thought of, but not
the appearance of orange at the poles.
You'd plugged it in to warm up at the centre
of the room. We sat on the floor, backs
resting against sofas, legs stretched
out towards each other, our tea
set down at our sides to brew.
How could I have
never seen a lava lamp? Never at my parents',
relations', neighbour's, or friend's, was I
ever illuminated by a marvel like this.
How had I
never heard Joni's *Blue*? Heard of her, but not
the album, had only listened to the Judy Collins' too
bright cover of "Both Sides Now."
I'd followed
Motown, the Beatles, several English rock stars, minor
seventies supergroups, but somehow missed
songs are like perfume.
We barely spoke.
Primal shapes formed and reformed, joined
and resisted combining. They fell
and rose according to an internal fire. Plant life,
dried then steeped, passed into our bodies:
rose, hibiscus, peppermint, chamomile—
it was all this I would describe
for years afterwards, not how our friendship grew
from that night, not how you became
a potter or me a traveller.
When meeting other
owners of these vessels devised from bright
spheres or admirers of this genie from Fort MacLeod—
I'd recount: lights out, herbal tea, red planets,
my big friend Kenneth, *you know I've been to sea before.*

Down to You

I trampled those days, a lion, believed
in myself with a ferocity that has since
never been the same. They were days
when self-knowing became real, a dented
bud of a tulip infused with its own
fragility and what it might reveal.
I'd discovered *Great Men*. This late
in the century, in so vast a country, so
few gay poets. On my invitation, you
read for the university's first gay
pride week. The dance that night,
dining tables upended, chairs stacked
in corners, nervous men and women
from town mixed with students. I dressed
in what I hoped gay men might wear. You
asked my straight friend to dance, he tried
not to show how proud he was not to
be an oaf, and when it was our turn, after
odd late-eighties tracks and disco throw-
backs: *everything you held high and told
yourself was true*. It was my first dance
with another man, my right hand
awkward upon your hip. You told me
it was your favourite Joni Mitchell song.
We glided, slow-motion skaters, on that
cafeteria's hardwood floor, the man I
would become blooming in the distance,
pairs of men and pairs of women in our
orbit, dim lights suspended from the old
rafters above. *As the days come down to you.*

A Half

A first for everything: the touch
down on the old island, the tube
ride to the hostel, though two
kind blokes offered a mattress,
pointed me to *FF*. I wasn't drawn
to the shaved heads of pale
Londoners but to an imposter
Englishman, an American football
jersey across his wide shoulders.
You've never tried it, mate?
You really should.
But he was careful, this devil gave
me only a half. *Your first time.*
Pressed it into my hand.
What I wonder now:
what if it had worked?
As when I discovered a taste
for fine food and never looked
back. I was twenty-two, open
to the world, I felt
as if I had sculled a tall
flute of champagne and though
I did try to kiss that faux
athlete, something
would tell me later my first
ecstasy hadn't worked.

Spacecakes

No Dutch knew the way. A proclivity desired by any
to whom it was unavailable. Yet, finally, a referral:
the Amsterdam Inn. Through a crunch of travellers.
Five guilders each. We bought three. Nervous of border
checks, the pungence! The oily paper bag placed
in the next compartment's empty baggage rack, the train
tumbling us across German, then Danish borders.
We snuck back into our college, a pledge between us:
would anyone guess our planned new knowledge?
First taste: nothing. Too impatient, we washed down
the carob, wheat, and smoky mulch with Tubørg beer
from the round platforms of the cafeteria vending
machine, the neck of the bottle offered to my willing
hand. Suddenly, my head the bouncing dot of a TV
sing-along, me zooming from one comic panel
to the next, my body catching up later, our other
classmates unaware (drunk they thought). For them
a perfect imitation of Estonian Andrüs. Uproarious
laughter at my jolly thick Baltic English, my secret:
I *was* Andrüs—before wandering off to tongue
a bisexual Brazilian boy but with no later physical
memory of it. I toured hallways and school lawns
and slept without knowing. Morning, and I shook
my skull, rattling marvel, the chain fell off my bicycle,
I rolled intact into the train station for Copenhagen.
My handwriting shimmered, the postcard floated
off radioactive and that afternoon, a John Hiatt
songbook from the Helsingør public library. Is this
what addiction is? To sing notes effortlessly off
unfamiliar pages, the accompaniment virtuosic;
to want to be like this always, so much shinier
than my sober self, my fingers automatic, a voice
new to me and this country, slicing the air into bits,
savoury and sweet. But my hunger was filled for days.

special k

i.

In London, I'd heard how clubbers stand in the middle
or at the dance floor's edge, unable to move, minds
active somewhere high above, unable
to converse with their bodies. I'd imagined thin
trails of drool leaking from one side
of their mouths. I understood e, its joy, but why
this?

So, when offered it for the first time by my new
friend of ten minutes, he laughed, "Oh no, it's not like
coke or anything, you only take the smallest spoonful,"
and he showed me his tiny vial and miniature
spoon and said "Trust me."

It's the same thing
I'd later suggest to dozens of friends, some who now
have their own bump bottles, and to one who had me
show him precisely how much, it was
the first time I said "Never overdo it,
trust me, just the littlest bit, block one
nostril, inhale in one quick pull, and wait."

ii.

Floating. The best is on top of e and you're light, can't
feel your body, only your head. Stairs are a problem
flat surfaces turn into steps and platforms. Direction is
lost even if you've just entered the hall: darkness
stretches out all around you, exits could be anywhere.

k without e, I am clear, bright and giddy as if
inhaling champagne and exhaling it through my skin.
I am a dancing devil, Tasmanian.

Another level: k-land. Music tinny and distant.
Silence in your heart, inside your lungs.
Flesh takes on greenish tones, faces distort.
Monsters drive you to stick as close
as possible to the friends you've come with,
all of you know exactly what the others feel.

Once a friend became the dictator of a new country
advised by cows who sent edicts through the speakers.
I saw numbers tumbling down on screens in front of me,
a rip-off from the *Matrix*, new realities cut into old
like badly edited video, each scene the same.
I tried to explain what I fathomed of all of this.
I made perfect sense to myself; my friends fled.

Even now I'm not sure if I comprehend what a k-hole is.
Maybe not everyone has out-of-body experiences.

Will I ever leave this state?
Still:
Wonderful.

Plane

i. long-haul

Flying: propelled like particles lifting into a
sneeze from a runway of lungs, part biology,
part impulse: I am always trying to get away.
Do kids have Spirograph these days? Plastic
shapes you stick to a board with pins, the
edges notched like zippers, disks you fit into
them, a pen stuck in the hole and your hand
guided to draw intricately enmeshed designs.
This is how I envision patterns of flight, remotely
controlled by computers, crisscrossing time
and geography, nights and days, filling the skies
as we increase destinations, yet avoid mishap—
in the air at least: a catering truck somehow
mowing into the side of my outbound plane
from Sydney, its panels beyond repair. I am
rerouted, layovers elongating my journey
one and a half times. The new plane has also
buckled somewhere in its history, the plastic
surrounding my window is warped. Through
a gap, I see part of the skeleton: some form
of moulding and insulation with a serial number
stamped across it. This kind of space scares me.
I think about limits: those we rarely notice—
the curve of the bulkhead, the width of these
aisles. Those that make themselves known—
the one-hundred and ninety-nine minutes
of battery life during which I write this in light
and bytes instead of ink. A methodology of meal
service: carts of wine and salad, meat entrées,
packaged snacks. I always leave the tiny packet
of butter, afraid it will slot in somewhere near
where my appendix was removed at age nine
(the year I got fat, one excuse for vanity's layover).

I wonder if they recycle it. Still, I remain lucky:
upgraded to Royal Executive Class all the way
from Australia to Frankfurt. I have never sat
on the jet's top floor: so much leg room. A sad,
new lesson of travelling —what I'm missing—
rather than the usual self-education: the length
of time our bodies will stay in one position,
our tolerance and fondness for ascending ages
of toddlers, all the ways we entertain ourselves,
the size of our bladders, the angles of our sleep.

ii. short-haul

So jealous are we of those who know our cities from the air,
the true colours of the roofs and sand, basins and scrub,
the armies of houses pushing against ironbark woodlands.
We turn our necks towards the windows wondering
if the wind's patterns on the ocean are found elsewhere
in our lives. I am transfixed by a hole in the shirt
of a man sitting one row ahead and across the aisle.
Will it be rent larger by speed or wear? Catch on
something like a thorn or his own stubborn nature?
Or back in the same assigned seats in five years, will
the coast below appear much like it does now, the hole
rent slightly wider, flesh chilled by the recirculating
air, more of it showing for anyone who cares to look.

Sukhimvit Soi 5

The taxis nudge you onto the walkway,
where else do automobiles flirt so
closely with you, you picture your toes
(wrapped in fake Birkenstocks, ten
dollars at the MBK Centre) crushed, but
who would notice—not the sellers of spicy
soups, barbecued skewers, deep-fried insects
(twenty baht for photos, less to eat them),
nor the *farang* with their new-found
girlfriends. All around the world we sell
ourselves but are more obvious here, buyers
(drinking Singha beer in Pussy Passage)
more plentiful. On Sukhimvit, deaf vendors
converse, punch numbers into calculators:
paintings on velvet, laser-etched crystal,
polyester boxer shorts advertised as silk,
magic tricks. Think: what do you need?
What do you want? It's probably cheap
but they pinch your skin for every
baht they can. Your white T-shirt turns
grey in the exhaust, congestion constricts
your throat —the hotel air conditioning
makes you sick — *buy it, buy it* (it may
be more costly than at home). Give change
to the legless beggar with the surprising
English, don't flinch when a young man
(*DVD-sexy movie-DVD-sexy movie*) or country
girl grabs at your elbow, nor complain if
internet costs are half elsewhere in the city.
You're a captive market, the pulsating noise
lassoes you, you can't even hide in your room,
sprawled across your mattress that beats
in time with the clichéd bar music below
that can't believe sleep is all you're after.

Dismayed

I am dismayed I have so little memory:
a mountain lost its top, an uninformed
tourist surrendered his eyeglasses to
a monkey in Ubud, there's carelessness
but also stupidity, a mouthful of clouds
I have been told is delicacy and I
choke instead. I am appalled I am so
very needy; a transitional economy
lacking political leadership, a bright
child starved of opportunity, the simple
round O of hunger, my shiny avarice.
I am galled at what I get away with,
small-brained and grasping, shallow
as weak light, a misplaced battery unable
to spark energy, it's the same story,
the one I try to forget, the one I give
in to but pretend I don't, it's what
I never say, what I never tell anyone
before lying down for a nap I don't need.

Lonely Planet

Land of smiles, the airport exhorts. Planes spit
out weary travellers, oxygen-starved, circadian
rhythms arrhythmic. Occasional gritty reports
do nothing to sate your friends' envy of business
junkets. You check in, achy and nauseous,
sleep clutching at more sleep. You wander
the crowded pavement, ask strangers' counsel until:
EMAIL the sign shouts, the lone
terminal surprising you. He's sent you a letter,
compressed down into pulse and signal
reassembled in the corner of a random hotel lobby.

It's about this separation; I find it hard to say.
Can we discuss?

You've been stretching the idea of a long-distance
relationship, a canvas over a frame but the scene
undecided: him in Canada, you usually in Australia,
now Bangkok.
He'll never know this
world but does it make a difference?
Beggars and tourists, tailors of custom-made
suits, windows filled with the finest
Thai silk, a parade of taxis in lemon, lime
and cherry chrome, a pack of motorcyclists idling
at the lights.
Alone and work-burdened
you type

This is just not the time.

and stagger into the fetid afternoon—
sewage, charcoal, exhaust—step through
vendors of wristwatches, sunglasses, CDs,
wooden curios, blackened skewers of chicken
and pork, durian, flower garlands ribboned in red.

He astonished you once by knowing when you
woke and slept halfway around the world.
Now: no redemption, this week is
the beginning of the end of everything.

Nearby, tuk-tuk drivers court passengers with
the promise of inside information. Stray dogs doze
smugly (Buddhists won't harm them, leave rice
on doorsteps.) At Wat Po, Buddha magnificently
reclines. Farther away: a Thai massage, an exotic
meal, a clever souvenir.
Small rewards,
but not necessarily the ones you were looking for.

Speaking Your Poetry Aloud

Oath

Just before the time we all gather for Christmas, the first time
in five years, my brothers and I fret over our father's health.
He can't keep away from mother's baking or, worse, the marbled
fat of beef brisket, the layer glistening beneath the crackling
rind of whole roasted pork, the greasy skin of chicken. Bacon.
Ham. We know how he is because this is how we are,
but young enough not to feel their effects.
                                                                        Still we gather
defects intact, as if we were unwrapping a new board game,
pieces missing, yet bothersome to return: Walter's poor
sight, my allergies, the keyhole in Tom's heart. What next?
We go for regular tests for the glaucoma and diabetes
settling into father late in his life.
                                                            What really frightens
us are his relatives, our relatives dropping like, well, dead
relatives: Eugene suddenly from stomach tumour, Uncle Bill,
his in his spine, Aunty Coral from the cancer she kept secret.
Even Dai Mo, great-auntie, not a blood relative, who gave us
our Chinese names, she passed on that season.

It is after midnight and hot when Tom rolls us a joint.
He'd checked before; we see each other so little who can
be sure, except we are brothers, were handed down related
taste glands (see *fatty meats* above). I smoked on occasion
in Europe, Walter keeps his in his freezer in Victoria.
This is good stuff, Tom says. *It's from Maui.* The first hit
leaves Walter playing video games in front of the computer.
Tom and I go out to explore, neighbourhood dogs smell us
and yelp, we tread on sleeping grass that curls in on itself.
A plumeria bloom falls to earth but it's too dark to see it.
It's up to me, his voice crackly with smoke, *You guys*
aren't going to do it, laughs. He's right. It's not impossible
but I don't want to and Walter feels too old, would only

parent with the right man. *How long is Dad going to last?*
(though he'll keep going, his siblings dying before him.)
He should hold a grandchild before he's gone.

Our eyes
water from the fumes inside our bodies, that glazed-over stoned look when everything is as plain as it's ever going to get, chemicals entering our bloodstreams, burnt carbon circling in our lungs, dead relatives, a promise, and us: alive.

Brother

Frankly I never thought you'd make it into a poem:
distant brother, sporty brother—not only older
and straighter, but some completely new species,
the only party in our family able to negotiate normalcy:
a taste for brand names, an occasional cigarette, a circle
of friends also jovial, energetic, misbehaved in expected
ways.
                    Your only secret a slightly malfunctioning
heart. The doctor said it spoke out of time. A murmur.
Un mur: a wall in French. So doubled: two walls?
Not solid enough. Whispering got through.
What happened? Did it heal over? No one
spoke of it again. Years later, like fabled debt
collectors, the doctors return with a new diagnosis:
Hodgkin's disease. Lymphoma.
                                                  You know neither
the man nor his illness, relieved phase two can be cured.
Your wife buoys your temper, jokes her morning
sickness is sharper than your swollen nodes.
Playing with knives. Do you remember? *Feel this,
it tickles.*
                    You ran the knife edge across my skin.
Red astonishment. Our eyes widened.
Thirty years later you say the same words:
Don't worry. We'll be OK. My nod also the same.
Our pact long ago, brothers. We told no one.

orbit

my latest family joke
father slowing down
mother speeding up
will they miss
each other mid-orbit

a vacation outing
a low wall of lava rock
near kauai's coughing surf
mother springs over
father stumbles sideways
in slow motion

when he rises
a thin wet handkerchief
of blood soaks
through the sleeve
of his skin

lucky father's bones
aren't brittle
like relatives
from mother's side
his family falling
apart from the inside
cancer of this
of that

my wilful forgetting
meant to create
a moving target
how can it strike
if I won't
let it be named

now blood flows
hot red
flesh opened
in three places
a sour trinity

mother looks back
not wanting to fuss
sinks out of sight

father closes his eyes tight
shuttered creases
so stars show behind them

face serene and slightly
unfocused as if
just returned
from a different planet

Succulent

Cocktails at a birthday celebration:
What kind of writing do you do?
I write poetry.
We change topics quickly.

She explains instead the difference
between succulents and other plants:
they make chlorophyll at night,
leaves, stems, and roots evolved to hoard
water while they bask all day in the sun.

Isn't that right? she says, nudging
her gardener-boyfriend.
What do you write about? Relationships?
No, I'm laughed at enough.

The attraction of succulents is not
only that they are the sole
plants wily enough to outwit my natural
ability to kill them
(my relationship is ending, too
quietly—as if its roots weren't taking
or it isn't on the right windowsill).

Shoots of hot sunlight cut through my skin
each time I observe a fierce doubling
in size, follow all twists and turns
towards heat and whatever is bright.

These are plants we tend not to call anything,
their complicated Latin nomenclature beyond us.
Yet they flourish in spite of my fascination,
neglect, and sadness. Fat and full of life.

Explaining too much

I blame your father that he stole any belief you might have
in yourself, he beat you as if threshing rice: years after
you left, raw grains spilled out on the footpath since
you refuse to take taxis and hide your goods from barbarians
at the door. He left you with no affection for him
and godless and doubtful and lacking in every confidence.

You blame my mother that I run from homes as if they were
burning and busy myself constantly with knitted things
and shiny objects and fan the flames and cover myself
with blankets and roll around in the grass. My criticism is
hard as the beaks of roosters and I romanticize all things distant.

The problem is that I wanted to but couldn't, believed too
much in prophecy and did you no favours by testing myself.
I introduced you to certain vices, nicer friends than the ones
you had and also to your unused fine silver and crockery.
You taught me to push in my chair after leaving the table,
yank out nose hairs with my fingers and fall asleep to someone
else's breathing: common enough for others but to me, a revelation.

November, start of summer

i.

Thirty-eight degrees. Windless. Worse on the asphalt.
Any hotter and rails would have buckled. Trains ran
slow that day. If I start with the weather, it's to pretend
it's not always with myself. Though here's my complaint:
unlike nimble Jack, I fell on the candlestick, it not only
penetrated me, but the wick is growing, twisting up
around my spine through my ribs looking for escape.
So I went to one of those dark places that most gay men
don't tell their straight friends about, pounded the maze's
corridors, and forgot the sun outside. Sisyphus trod
up and down; our punishment is circular, chasing one
another's tails. At last, someone turned around. He had
the most un-gay hair I'd ever seen. Poofs are coiffed
with product, or shaved short, but his thick ruddy
coils high on his scalp, almost hid the rest of him.
I couldn't coax him into a cubicle. He'd been inside
for hours and was spent. But I sank my hand into
those burnt red cords and pulled him like an anchor
to my mouth, and we kissed, clanging against
the lockers and groping each other. The wick emerged
from my right ear and was lit by his crimson hair.

ii.

The next day I felt lifted and light
and forced to notice I was something
called happy, which made me realize
I hadn't been the whole month before.
I'd thought what I needed was some
rumpy-pumpy, hip-swinging action
to stop me thinking. But sex mixed
with desperation or compromise
can make things worse. A kiss was
enough. On my cycle home from work
I saw strings of shoes laced together
and thrown over telephone wires, a man
playing soccer with his mutt, two men
in the middle of a sidewalk trying to
put socks on a girl. A spent jacaranda
flower fell from a high branch. I rode
towards it, let it hit me in the face.

Marijuana Fudge Cake

i. new year's retreat

Six days to treasure, to trace the shape of
with my thumb. Let rooms rest that had
allowed too little light, my failed
domesticity. I inhaled the coastal heat,
the company of fine men, our unstructured
eating. The house half alive with huntsman
spiders, crane flies, fingernail-sized frogs;
the veranda's opening stitched together
with silver web; pollen and twigs woven
into carpets. A magpie flew into its
reflection. Two toy poodles pranced in
perfect circles. I scrubbed off dead
hair and skin, drank cheap Riesling, ate
marijuana fudge cake. An astrologer
forecast my year ahead as the worst
of times; these early days—still and lop-eared—
I swallowed without chewing, danced
a high-kneed jig, grass fingers scratching
the skin of my ankles, air so fresh
it made me nauseous and short of breath.

ii. rebounding

The second of January after a night
of e, k, dancing and libido
we drank morning and afternoon.
More pleasure, I figured *why not?*
the confection swallowed
I didn't expect rebounding
in my head between
constructs of tires and rubber bands.
I'd charged past the cake's light
silliness into this flat, dead
space as if atlases were
piled on my shoulders and torso
covering me whole. I stayed
on the steps of the veranda
until the sky drained of obvious
light, squinted at a map
of the southern night
but when the candle flame got
bright enough, my eyes lost
sight of the stars.
Orion was still easy,
Lepus a faint hexagon.
Beyond, all the rest bled
into one. Astronomers' follies.
I was stoned but I knew
they should be bright.
The third of January,
I thought of all
the people I'd met on my
island continent and how
little I knew them.
I went ring- and shoeless for a week.

The Gentle Man

Honour the gentle man,
his death in front of a
suburban train. He might
have slipped clean away
into life if not for timing
if not for a schoolboy
with fifteen hours of
grog in his blood.

Came upon the gentle man
just past noon who'd
come from a surprise
party, now changing
train lines, alone
at the station, end seat
of the platform, no station
master on duty. Privacy
perhaps he'd sought,
or quiet.

Fist raised at the gentle man
staggering out automatic
doors—*What the fuck are you
staring at?* Biceps round
as signals, a torso of metal
rail. The girls with him
a restraint: he broke free.

Pity the gentle man
the question asked again
the boy held back again
no matter, the man
jumped, ran for the other
platform, no matter.

Praise the gentle man
testaments tendered by
his lover and his sister
"record the gentle and
  loving nature of
  Christopher Harris."

Cry for the gentle man
Was he more scared
than we would be
to face down this
Rodney Kerr, days shy
of eighteen, now parole-
eligible in one quick
year, was this boy
scared—ever—the way
we are scared of boys
like him?

Accuse the gentle man
did drunk boy feel
himself a target
of desire direct or
faint as a sense of
someone standing
behind you.

Question the gentle man
"killed instantly": yes
or no? I've died many
deaths by Rodney Kerrs
stretched-out tracks
a railroad to
a far mountain.

Abandon the gentle man
the boy and the two girls
walked away—did they
care if he breathed
still?—the security camera
caught them
calm and unhurried.

Absolve the gentle man
did expletive boy at first
sight know the sweet
soft nature he hid or
could not hide?

Remember the gentle man
all of us might be him
alone on a platform.
Stand braced
for that fist to meet
with the bone in your chin
or miss, and rattle
off to another station.

Fine

Have you found your wings, Gabriel?
Some of us never get the hang
of life.
Others get the hang of it all
too well.
Selfish bastard, leaving Ian
with the cleanup. He'd suffered through
your last try too.
Now: the police
report, funeral arrangements, sorting
of objects.
You tired of pills to keep you
flying stable, took too many
of a different sort. Not a bad way
to go. I'm averse
to pain and would also choose
a long hard sleep
But why doze
with a voice like yours: a rolling
laughing tenor, wanting
to please, splashing through
the sad minor bits. Get me
to the dancing part.
When I saw you
last, you showed me the new
hipsters you'd designed and sewn
yourself, the hipbone of your thin
frame floating above its waistline.
Do you like them?
I love them.
Your smile radiant. Everything,
for a moment, fine.

Crystal

By all reports, it's ravaging lives, not
everyone's but enough to make you
pause and wonder about what we trade
for freedom—this modern hag casting
spells, incanting *your hunger will not cease*
till addicts lose jobs, friends, everything.
A gemstone of 51 facets reduced to
a pane of glass, a personality distilled
to base parts: aggression, fearlessness,
libido, speed.
                    But the only time I tried it
the lover-of-an-acquaintance supplier
said *that'll keep you up 'til tomorrow noon*
but all I felt was awaked-ness, the night a bit
more clear and focused, a mild itch
in my loins. The Melbourne eve was 35 degrees
and hotter than anything I'd felt
before, but ask anyone: that part is objective.

Stages of Gravity

i.

We rifle through the season's colours
dart in and out of smart shops
in the city centre—boutiques and
chain stores—in search of a dress.
Theressa explains the way fabrics
drape over bosoms and hips,
how a high waist would not suit
someone of Isabelle's height
(in one week she'd also gained
surprising weight). Not matronly
but not carefree or coquettish.
No. The shade was the key —
a deep purple or blue?
Green might contrast well
with her red hair. Nothing too
showy, though she'd be the centre
of attention. Her only certainty:
she does not want to wear black.

ii.

Melbourne is where we wait:
clearances, paperwork, phone calls,
flight arrangements, schedules,
different time zones. Vanuatu
lacked forensics—the autopsy
performed in Brisbane.

Here: Isabelle,
your widow (such an old word!
how could this be?); Theressa, your boss—
dispatched to a new duty—and me,
an old friend, flown in from Sydney—
what else can I do? The
funeral in Canada will be too
far away, too sad.

When found, your face
and parts of your body had
blackened—where the blood
had pooled? Villagers called it
Black Magic, a young man dead
in his sleep, the prime of life.
La sorcellerie. Witchcraft —or the *kava*
you'd ingested the night before?

Theressa recounts every
theory, breaking the news, the last
terrible days. The girls take
turns at a puzzle, dissembled,
the pieces foreign, it's unclear:

how does a body get home?

iii

I force them out of their hotel room,
loan them my mobile phone,
listen, make jokes, bring takeout
Chinese food (MSG added, too oily).
In dress shops, I hush the sales
assistants who ask the occasion.

Surprisingly, you do not
hover around us, you are not
there. Yet it is about you,
as if we'd enter a room painted
in a colour unnecessary
to name afterwards.

Two days later,
the body ("we can't call him
'the body,'" Isabelle despairs)
is airplane-ready. There is no
place to cry. I pull
strings, get them seats in
business class they could not have
got themselves and, brushed
in my own colours
of dismay, I board my own
shorter flight home,
the bureaucracy of death
cleared—for now—blood
pooling low
in my calves and feet.

iv.

Everyone has a doppelganger, some have
many: one in each major North American
city or a few on each continent —
the populated ones at least. Imagine
yours dining at Zimi's, the bistro
next to my office, its front
wide open in summer
(a mouth breathing back and forth
the neighbourhood exhaust and chatter),
in winter its windows are slid shut,
reflections distorted floor to ceiling
inside and out.
It is winter.
His elbows on the table (is that still rude?)
Shoulders hunched, a long face
pressing forward, sand-coloured hair.
A small mouth above a narrow chin
in a half-smile while listening to conversation.
Remarkably, when he stands
he has your height and build: the angularity
of the tall, shoulders like the crossbeams
of a farm house, a coniferous not deciduous
torso.
His voice
I can't hear: it might break
the spell, your accent
comical, the tones too expressive for Anglo
flatlands, inflections in your low
baritone harder and quicker
in French alone.

I stand so long, his supper mates and he exit
through the glass doors, loiter in poses
of farewell. I can't control my feet taking me
forward, the wind off the lake sifting through
pines, my hands gripping the points of his
elbows. Gracefully, he allows me this
gesture. I rest my forehead against his chest.

V.

At another memorial, far earlier,
you grip my left elbow
as we enter the church,
I am overcome by tears—melodrama?
others who'd known her better
—like you, her ex—are
composed. "Wimp," you taunt
and briefly I come out of my haze.

After college, you are captured
in the loops and curves
of your script. How heartsick
we all are for each other, the grate
of your envelope through the mail
slot. I send back three neat stanzas.
You reply: "It was only a letter!"

Today, in Ottawa, near a stand
of massive pines, a monument
unveiled for aid workers who'd lost
their lives abroad. It feels right to
be staid and calm, but I break
down when I meet your mother's
eyes and she starts to cry.

Your family divides in two:
your tiny father with such tall
sons, a granddaughter bouncing
on his knee. What light you had
is his; your mother is filled
with gravity (her voice
on the phone: *of course*
we remember you).
From her, your sadness.

It is now your brother's and sister's;
it drowns me, wide as the river
its hard monotone just out of sight.
Your other sister is silent.

We walk through an archway
framed by two giant bronze feathers,
twin benches nearby. Again,
I weep inelegant tears and lean
on Mary Ellen, my nose fills
with wet and we ignore
a cameraman who asks if he can
catch questions on tape.
The assembled push towards
refreshments, commemoration
so different than celebration.

I am learning gravity but,
Jean-Pierre, we are students
no longer. If I were to leap
into the air like the youths
we once were, and hover
defying my inadequate
spindly feathers, could I

coax you out of hiding
to bring me to
ground
with a kind
                    sharp
                              word?

The Last Fathers

Distant fathers, stern fathers, fathers loving, fathers
arbitrary, absent fathers, fathers silent. A season
of import and displacement, forgetfulness and regret.
There were modest burials, also wailing and shouting,
sweetgrass fires. In the south of Germany, the most
abused daughter did not attend the funeral. The overseas
son bought chestnuts and roasted them. In Montreal,
the eight-year-old granddaughter was scolded: *Why
are you crying? Your father is alive.* In Ottawa, they feasted,
told stories: it had been a long illness. In accordance
with tradition, the daughter cut off her long dark hair,
the young grandson stoked embers the night through.
I'm not even sure where the last father lived. His son
only wrote of the news and after, there was quiet.

Speaking Your Poetry Aloud

Breathe a mixture of elements, at least some
oxygen added. Forget the unpaid bill,
the text message from Mom. Stare into the
crowd. Know you've got something
they want. Then own it, call it home.
Sing out of every complex cell. Music
finds its way, a hermit crab skipping
from an outgrown shell to one that fits.

Advice I got on road-crossing in Hanoi:
find a gap in traffic, slip in, stride at a steady
pace across the road, no sudden movements,
don't rush or panic, the motorbikes
and cars will find their way around you.
When it's dusk, cross as if this is the last
step you'll take, the click of your feet as they hit
the ground, a metronome for your use alone.

Let it all hover in the air like fireflies
released from a jar, your mother's caught you—
release release their light is no good dead
see them pirouette, rearranging
their constellations, even if you have never
known fireflies and this analogy is misplaced.
Silently watch them a few seconds then bow
your head just so, everything seems better.
That they're now outside, punctuating
sentences the night is writing freehand.

Insured

QUAN Announcing the arrival of Jeremiah Akira Lopaka Quan, born 3:52 am (HST) December 15, 2002, to Kimiko and Tom Quan of Kahaluu, Hawaii. Thrilled Grandparents are Joe and Hilda Quan (Vancouver) and Matsue Fukayama (Fukuoka, Japan). Proud Uncles are Walter (Victoria) and Andy Quan (Sydney, Australia) and Tomohiko Fukayama (Yokohama, Japan). A new playmate for Wasabi. Insured.

I need it explained.

My eldest brother, Walter, is placing a birth announcement.
Monday is a pittance—twenty dollars—compared
to Saturday's eighty. *Why not Monday to Thursday?* I suggest.
One each day. It's how my mind works. Walter will
err against our *pah-kay*-ness, our proud frugality
where the word *Chinese* is shorthand for cheap.
It will go in the weekend edition, which our parents,
their contemporaries, and Walter scan—
obituaries mainly, a careful glance at the rest.

He's only seven years older than I am, how did I slip
onto this side of the generation gap? I rarely buy
newspapers, stay informed through TV, not radio, mostly
the internet. Friends, colleagues, check property prices;
not me, at most I browse personal ads in the local gay rag.

Insured? I email. *I don't get it.* But it's another in-joke,
a created tradition, ours ended this way, why not
our nephew's? Insurance men used to comb through
birth announcements to sell new policies. My father's
generation headed them off at the pass,
a pre-emptive No Thank You, the first lesson
in the life of a newborn: ward off strangers' greed.

Still, *insured* is not inaccurate—our parents giddy
at their first grandchild, the family name surviving
against chance. This swaddled joy, some magic
word—our faith in it—touched to his brow.

Acknowledgements

I would like to thank the editors of the following journals where some of these poems (sometimes under other titles and in slightly different forms) have previously appeared: "Smelt" and "Orbit"in *Asia Literary Review*; "Reprimand," "Wings," and "Aftertaste" in *Journal of Australian Studies*; "Oath" *in Meanjin*. "The Gentle Man" and "Crystal" appeared in the anthology, *Seminal: The Anthology of Canada's Gay Male Poets*, John Barton and Billeh Nickerson, editors. (Arsenal Pulp Press, 2007).

I would also like to acknowledge Michael Farrell, Jill Jones, and David Edler for their thoughtful advice on the manuscript.

I have greatly appreciated the opportunity to read some of these poems to attentive listeners and fellow poets at the Loft Readings at the University of Technology Sydney, organized by Berndt Sellheim; Perverse Verse, organized by Gail Hewison of the Feminist Bookstore in Sydney; and the Sydney Poetry Seminar, organized by Peter Minter.

To the family members, friends, lovers, acquaintances, and strangers who appear in these poems, both my gratitude and apologies.

My poetry has often been inspired and spurred on by the work of other poets, from around the world, too many to mention, but to whom I honour their dedication to this art, their singing. Editing is also an art and I'm greatly indebted to John Barton, as fine an editor as poet, for his hard work and high standards. Kudos to designer, Terry Gallagher, for a great cover. A respectful nod to publisher, Karen Haughian, for allowing me to share these words with the world.

And to you who have read my poems into life, my thanks as well, dear reader.

www.andyquan.com